20TH CENTURY SCIENCE AND TECHNOLOGY

1960s

SPACE AND TIME

Please visit our web site at: www.garethstevens.com
For a free color catalog describing Gareth Stevens' list of high-quality books and
multimedia programs, call 1-800-542-2595 (USA) or 1-800-461-9120 (Canada).
Gareth Stevens Publishing's Fax: (414) 332-3567.

Library of Congress Cataloging-in-Publication Data

Parker, Steve.
    1960s: space and time / by Steve Parker. — North American ed.
        p. cm. — (20th century science and technology)
    Includes bibliographical references and index.
    ISBN 0-8368-2945-X (lib. bdg.)
    1. Science—History—20th century—Juvenile literature. 2. Technology—
History—20th century—Juvenile literature. [1. Science—History—20th century.
2. Technology—History—20th century. 3. Technological innovations.
4. Inventions—History—20th century.] I. Title.
Q125.P3254   2001
509.046—dc21   2001020785

This North American edition first published in 2001 by
Gareth Stevens Publishing
A World Almanac Education Group Company
330 West Olive Street, Suite 100
Milwaukee, WI 53212 USA

Original edition © 2000 by David West Children's Books. First published in Great Britain
in 2000 by Heinemann Library, Halley Court, Jordan Hill, Oxford OX2 8EJ, a division
of Reed Educational and Professional Publishing Limited. This U.S. edition © 2001 by
Gareth Stevens, Inc. Additional end matter © 2001 by Gareth Stevens, Inc.

Designers: Jenny Skelly and Aarti Parmar
Editor: James Pickering
Picture Research: Brooks Krikler Research

Gareth Stevens Editor: Valerie J. Weber

Photo Credits:
Abbreviations: (t) top, (m) middle, (b) bottom, (l) left, (r) right

Corbis: pages 4(t), 5 all, 6(b), 10(l), 10-11(t), 11 all, 14 both, 15(t), 16-17(m), 16-17(b), 17(t),
    18(b), 19(t), 20(r), 22(m), 22-23(t), 23(b), 23(t), 24-25(b), 25(t), 26(t), 27(tl), 28(bl), 28-29(t).
Corbis, Corbis Images: cover.
Corbis Images: pages 8(t), 9(t), 12(ml), 12(mr), 14-15.
David West: pages 17(b), 29(t), 29(b).
Hulton Getty Collection: pages 4(b), 7(r), 16(l), 18(t), 20(l), 20 both, 22(b), 24-25(t), 27(tr), 27(bl).
NASA: pages 12(tr), 12(bl).
Novosti: page 15(b).
Science & Society: page 29(m).
Solution Pictures: pages 8(b), 16-17(t).

Printed in the United States of America

1 2 3 4 5 6 7 8 9 05 04 03 02 01

20TH CENTURY SCIENCE AND TECHNOLOGY

1960s

SPACE AND TIME

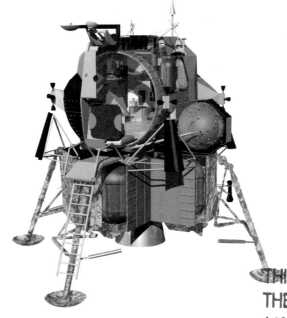

Steve Parker

Gareth Stevens Publishing
A WORLD ALMANAC EDUCATION GROUP COMPANY

CONTENTS

In 1960, the laser was invented — a pure, concentrated, powerful source of light. Within a few years, lasers could be used in hundreds of different ways.

THE SPACE RACE

The 1960s will always be remembered for the space race. The two world superpowers — the United States and the Soviet Union (now mainly Russia) — competed against each other for space firsts: to put a person into orbit around Earth, to launch more and better satellites, to build space stations, to send probes to distant planets, and perhaps the greatest achievement of all, to land astronauts on the Moon. Amazingly, all of this happened during the 1960s. Being first was not the only goal at stake, however. Each huge nation also foresaw how it could use space for military purposes by orbiting spy satellites and possibly even missiles of mass destruction.

During the decade, the rush for supremacy in space drove scientific research and technological invention at a great pace. Spin-offs from space and military programs flooded into everyday life, ranging from live color television beamed around the world by satellites and sight-saving laser eye surgery to plastic clothes and non-stick coatings on frying pans.

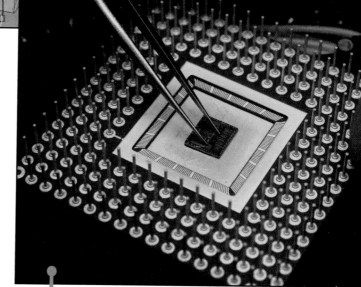

The push to make electronic circuits smaller led to the invention of the first microchips in about 1967.

In 1961, the USSR put the first person in space. In 1962, John Glenn was the third U.S. astronaut in space and the first to orbit Earth.

Telstar 2 was an early communications satellite, relaying phone calls and television channels.

New, cheap plastic materials encouraged bold and daring fashions like see-through, disposable dresses.

A MATTER OF SIZE

During the 1910s, scientists had split atoms, proving that these were not the smallest nor the most basic particles of matter. Atoms were composed of even tinier bits, such as electrons, protons, and neutrons. By the 1960s, new evidence from more powerful particle accelerators, or atom smashers, pointed to even smaller particles than these.

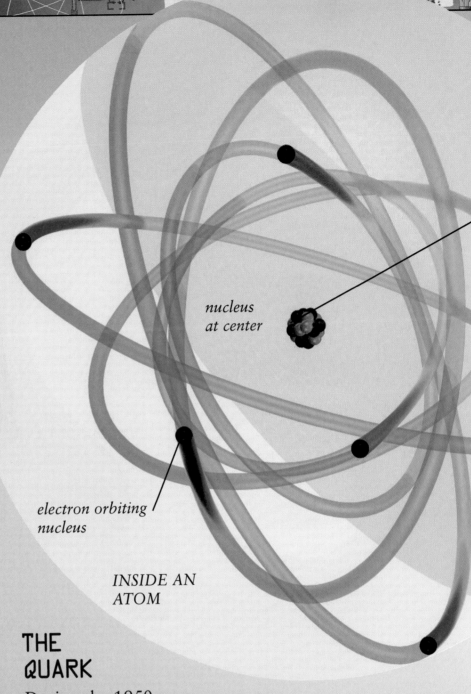

nucleus at center

electron orbiting nucleus

INSIDE AN ATOM

THE QUARK

During the 1950s, American physicist Murray Gell-Mann studied cosmic rays and found that strange particles in them did not follow the usual laws of atomic physics. Gell-Mann proposed a new way of organizing these particles into eight families. In 1964, experiments proved this theory, showing that protons, neutrons and similar particles were made of even smaller pieces — quarks.

Murray Gell-Mann (b. 1929) became a professor of theoretical physics in 1956 and received a Nobel Prize in physics in 1969.

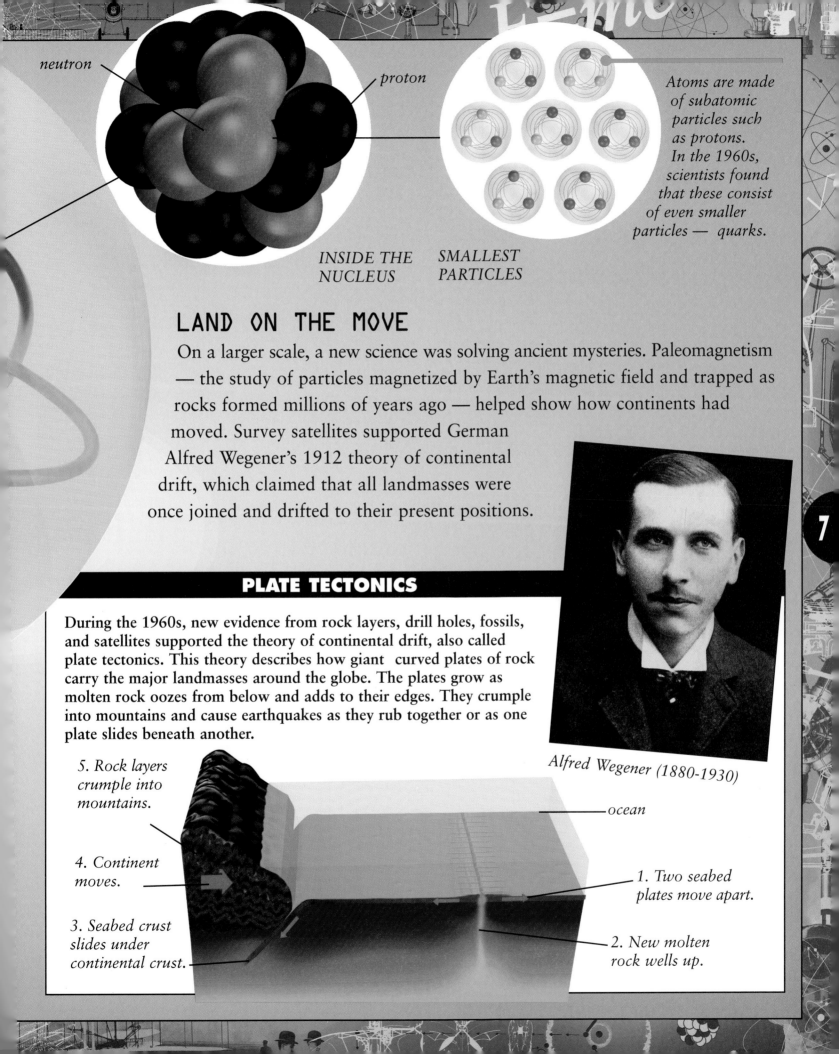

neutron

proton

INSIDE THE NUCLEUS

SMALLEST PARTICLES

Atoms are made of subatomic particles such as protons. In the 1960s, scientists found that these consist of even smaller particles — quarks.

LAND ON THE MOVE

On a larger scale, a new science was solving ancient mysteries. Paleomagnetism — the study of particles magnetized by Earth's magnetic field and trapped as rocks formed millions of years ago — helped show how continents had moved. Survey satellites supported German Alfred Wegener's 1912 theory of continental drift, which claimed that all landmasses were once joined and drifted to their present positions.

PLATE TECTONICS

During the 1960s, new evidence from rock layers, drill holes, fossils, and satellites supported the theory of continental drift, also called plate tectonics. This theory describes how giant curved plates of rock carry the major landmasses around the globe. The plates grow as molten rock oozes from below and adds to their edges. They crumple into mountains and cause earthquakes as they rub together or as one plate slides beneath another.

Alfred Wegener (1880-1930)

5. Rock layers crumple into mountains.

4. Continent moves.

3. Seabed crust slides under continental crust.

ocean

1. Two seabed plates move apart.

2. New molten rock wells up.

UP THERE

As the superpowers raced to launch astronauts, astronomers peered through telescopes across the Universe and analyzed the mass of information from new satellites and space probes.

RADIO ASTRONOMY

Radio telescopes detect natural radio and similar waves coming from the sky. These invisible rays provide information about objects deep in space. In 1963, radio astronomers noticed an incredibly powerful source of radio and other waves far across the Universe. It seemed no bigger than an average star yet gave out more energy than 100 whole galaxies. It was called a quasar, matter and energy falling into a giant black hole at the center of a galaxy.

A pulsar flashes on and off like a lighthouse but sends out radio waves instead of light waves. It is a fast-spinning neutron star, the dense core of an old star that has exploded.

UFO FEVER

Regular radio blips from pulsars fueled ideas of aliens in space. Might they visit Earth? Many UFOs (unidentified flying objects) were photographed, and "UFO fever" gripped the world. Although some were hoaxes, others were natural weather features like ball lightning, and some were secret military test craft. As far as we know, none were alien spacecraft.

The UFO C-9, photographed in the 1960s

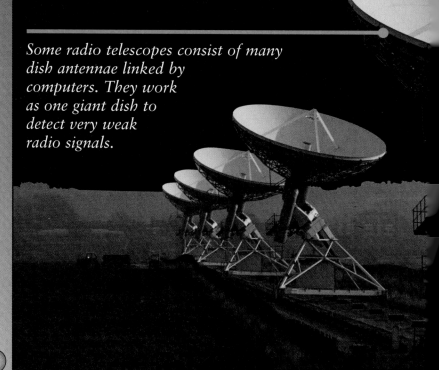

Some radio telescopes consist of many dish antennae linked by computers. They work as one giant dish to detect very weak radio signals.

8

BLIP, BLIP, BLIP, BLIP

In 1967, a huge radio telescope was built at the Mullard Radio Astronomy Laboratory in Great Britain. Within weeks, a team of researchers noticed strange, regular pulses of radio signals, 1.3 seconds apart, from far away in our galaxy. Alien signals? By the year's end, the team found another pulsing object. They discovered that the signals were emitted by fast-spinning neutron stars called pulsars — small, incredibly dense remnants of old giant stars that had collapsed into themselves. Since then, many more pulsars and quasars have been identified.

A quasar pours out unimaginable amounts of energy from the heart of a galaxy. Some quasars emit mainly light; others send out radio waves. They are among the most distant and powerful objects discovered so far.

RADIO TELESCOPES

Our eyes see light rays from the Sun, Moon, stars, planets, and other objects in space. Many other kinds of rays also reach Earth from space, however, including natural radio waves, cosmic rays, and microwaves. They are invisible to our eyes, but radio telescopes can detect them. Radio telescopes use antennae (aerials) shaped like large dishes, similar to huge satellite TV dishes, or long wires strung on towers to receive the signals. Radio astronomy began in the mid 1940s but expanded greatly in the 1960s.

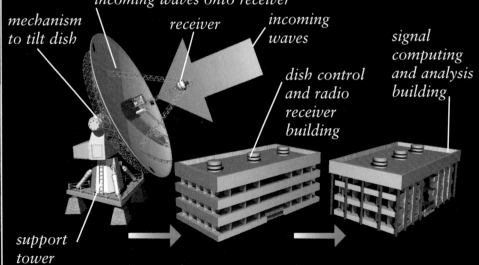

parabolic dish to reflect and concentrate incoming waves onto receiver

mechanism to tilt dish

receiver

incoming waves

dish control and radio receiver building

signal computing and analysis building

support tower

THE RACE IS ON

At the beginning of the 1960s, most experts agreed that the United States led the Soviet Union in space technology. It was a shock when the Soviets announced they had put the first human into space on April 12, 1961.

Soviet leader Khrushchev meets fellow communist leader Fidel Castro of Cuba in 1963.

THE COLD WAR

The Cold War was a tense stand-off: the capitalist United States and its allied Western nations versus the communist USSR and its Eastern European allies. The success of the first piloted space flight boosted the USSR's scientific reputation and its political system, led by Nikita Khrushchev.

During the Cold War, the USSR frequently displayed its military might. Intercontinental ballistic missiles, armed with nuclear warheads, could reach the other side of the world.

THE FIRST TRIP INTO SPACE

With the aid of four strap-on boosters, a Soviet A-1 rocket launched Gagarin's craft, *Vostok 1*. The capsule measured 7 1/2 feet (2.3 meters) across and weighed 2 2/3 tons (2.4 metric tons). It had few controls; the astronaut was primarily a passenger for the trip. *Vostok 1* reached a maximum height of 203 miles (327 kilometers) on its single-orbit journey. Its shield deflected the enormous heat of reentry as the craft plunged back into Earth's atmosphere at nearly 5,000 miles (8,000 km) per hour. A parachute slowed its final descent to the ground. At the time, the Soviets announced that Gagarin had stayed in his craft until landing, but he had really ejected about 4 miles (6 km) above Earth and parachuted down separately.

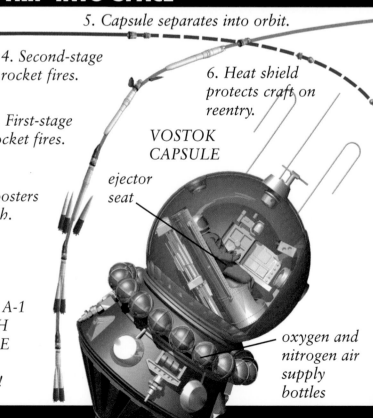

5. Capsule separates into orbit.

4. *Second-stage rocket fires.*

3. *First-stage rocket fires.*

6. *Heat shield protects craft on reentry.*

VOSTOK CAPSULE

ejector seat

2. *Boosters detach.*

SOVIET A-1 LAUNCH VEHICLE

1. *Liftoff!*

oxygen and nitrogen air supply bottles

In 1961, President John F. Kennedy declared the U.S. goal in space — to land a man on the Moon and bring him safely back by the end of the decade.

In 1961, President John F. Kennedy declared the U.S. goal in space — to land a man on the Moon and bring him safely back by the end of the decade.

FIRST IN SPACE

The first person in space was Yuri Gagarin, a former Soviet air force pilot. His craft, the ball-shaped *Vostok 1*, had already been used to carry Sputnik satellites and was tested in several unpiloted flights. Gagarin took off from Baikanour Space Center, made one orbit of Earth, and landed near the Volga River after a flight lasting 1 hour, 48 minutes.

John Glenn (b. 1921) made his first flight in a Mercury craft, Friendship 7. In 1998, he became the oldest astronaut when he went into space again on the space shuttle.

11

After his space trip, Gagarin (1934–1968) became director of the Soviet program to train women astronauts. He was due to return to space in a Soyuz craft when he was killed in a jet-fighter training accident.

7. Gagarin ejects from reentry capsule and lands by parachute.

A SWIFT REPLY

Stung by the Soviets' success, the United Sates soon shot its own astronauts into space. On May 5, 1961, Alan Shepherd took a 15-minute suborbital flight; 8 weeks later, Virgil Grissom took another. On the third trip, on February 20, 1962, John Glenn made three full Earth orbits. The space program's next goal — a craft capable of reaching the Moon.

ON THE MOON!

Although President Kennedy had died before his dream was realized, the United States reached its goal on July 20, 1969. For the first time, humans walked on another world — the Moon.

Apollo 11 *crew (from left): Neil Armstrong, Michael Collins, "Buzz" Aldrin*

APOLLO PROGRAM

The Moon landing was the climax of 10 years of incredible technological advances in almost all areas of science. Early, unpiloted Apollo space shots tested the vehicles and equipment. With *Apollo 7* in October 1968, astronauts went too, checking out all the procedures and equipment for a Moon landing.

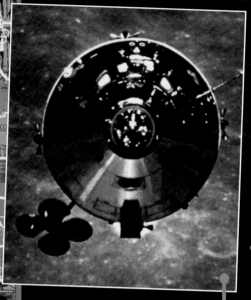

Collins in the Apollo 11 *Command Module stayed in Moon orbit.*

12

With the Lunar Module in the background, an astronaut salutes the U.S. flag on the Moon's surface.

A GIANT LEAP

Apollo 11 made that landing. Its commander, Neil Armstrong (*b. 1930*), stepped from the Lunar Module onto the gray, dusty surface, proclaiming "That's one small step for a man, one giant leap for mankind." The crew collected 55 pounds (25 kilograms) of lunar rocks and dust. The last Moon mission was *Apollo 17* in 1972. No one has set foot there since.

Apollo 13 crew splash down safely in 1970. Technical failures shortened their trip.

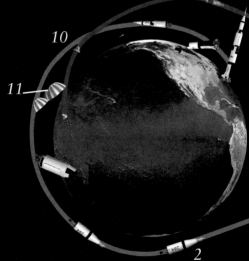

9

10

11

2

THE APOLLO MISSION

Atop the *Saturn V*, Apollo astronauts inhabited the Command Module (CM). This was attached to the Service Module (SM), except for final reentry to Earth. The Lunar Module (LM) detached from the CM to land on the Moon with two astronauts, and when done with its work, took off to rejoin the CM in Moon orbit.

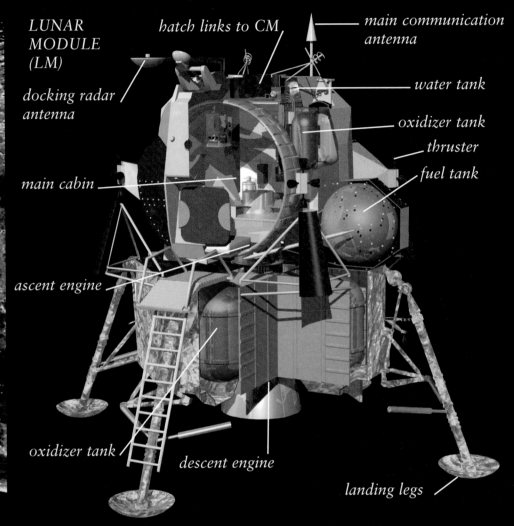

LUNAR MODULE (LM)

hatch links to CM

main communication antenna

docking radar antenna

water tank

oxidizer tank

thruster

fuel tank

main cabin

ascent engine

oxidizer tank

descent engine

landing legs

SATURN V

escape tower

Command Module

Service Module

Lunar Module

third-stage S-IVB

1 J-2 rocket engine

second-stage S-II

5 J-2 rocket engines

first-stage SIC

5 F-1 rocket engines

1. Apollo takes off.
2. Apollo leaves Earth's orbit.
3. LM docks with CM.

4. LM and CM flies for two days to Moon.
5. LM and CM enters Moon's orbit.

6. LM separates from CM and lands on the Moon.
7. LM leaves Moon and links up with CM.
8. CM leaves lunar orbit for Earth.
9. CM detaches from SM and enters Earth's orbit.
10. CM enters Earth's atmosphere.
11. Splashdown!

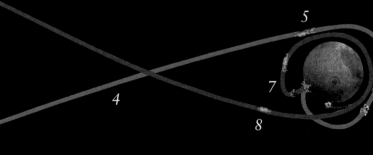

SATELLITE REVOLUTION

A satellite is now launched every week or two. In the 1960s, however, satellites were news; every launch made global headlines. Some, like the Telstar series and the *Early Bird* satellite, became almost like celebrities — as famous as the human stars of movies, sports, and popular music.

AN EYE ON THE WEATHER

The TIROS (Television and Infrared Observation Satellite) series of ten satellites, launched between 1960 and 1965, carried television cameras to photograph the clouds far below. They also detected the temperature at different heights above the ground. The information was radioed down to Earth and used to make the first satellite-aided weather forecasts.

14

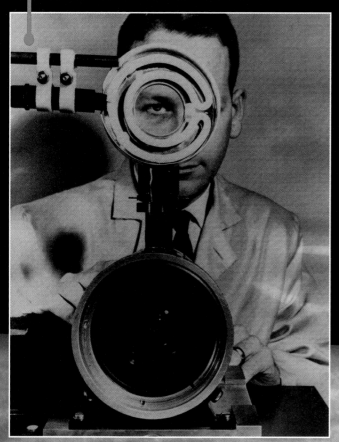

A technician tests one of the two television cameras on TIROS 10 *in 1965.*

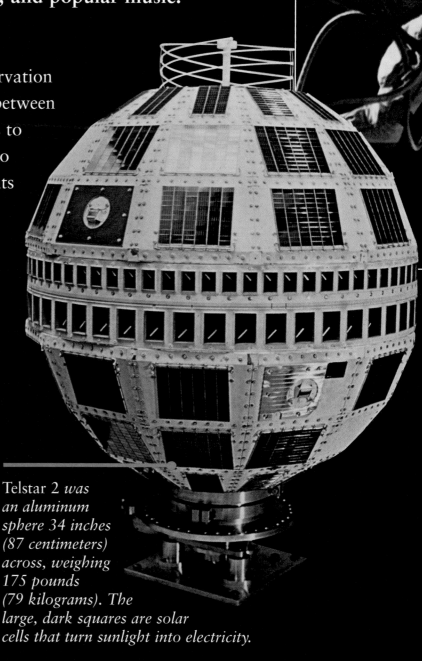

Telstar 2 *was an aluminum sphere 34 inches (87 centimeters) across, weighing 175 pounds (79 kilograms). The large, dark squares are solar cells that turn sunlight into electricity.*

Today, a small dish antenna can receive satellite TV. In the 1960s, huge dishes like Goonhilly in Britain picked up signals and passed them to television stations on land.

LIVE AT LAST

In July 1962, *Telstar 1* communication satellites sent live black-and-white television pictures from the United States to Europe. In May 1963, *Telstar 2* went one better and relayed the first live color television images across the Atlantic Ocean. Because the satellites were in low oval orbits, they could only be used for short periods, unlike today's television satellites.

Astronauts walk in space when their craft or satellites need repair. In 1965, Soviet Alexei Leonov was the first to space walk, soon followed by American Edward White, shown above.

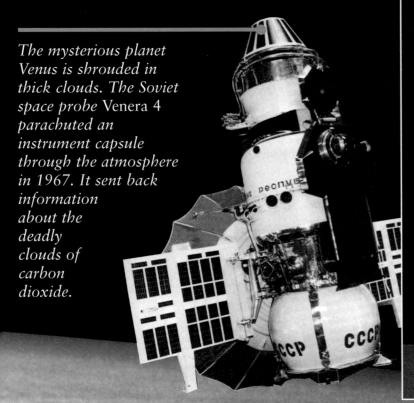

The mysterious planet Venus is shrouded in thick clouds. The Soviet space probe Venera 4 parachuted an instrument capsule through the atmosphere in 1967. It sent back information about the deadly clouds of carbon dioxide.

MISSION TO VENUS

1. Venera 4 is in orbit.

2. Descent capsule separates and enters Venus's atmosphere.

3. Parachute deploys.

4. Capsule caves in 15 miles (25 km) above Venus's surface.

Once *Venera 4* reached the orbit of Venus, its capsule detached and entered the atmosphere. A parachute opened to slow its descent, and its instruments switched on to start transmitting data back to Earth. It took 94 minutes before the massive atmospheric pressure crushed the capsule.

ON THE MOVE

No major new forms of transportation were invented during the 1960s, though 1969 saw the first flights of two very different aircraft. The Boeing 747 jumbo jet and the French-English jetliner Concorde suggested how long-distance air travel might evolve in different ways.

The submersible Trieste dived to nearly 7 miles (11 km) in 1960.

FAST VERSUS BIG

The Concorde was for rich people in a hurry. It crossed the Atlantic in about three hours, cruising at 1,348 miles (2,170 km) per hour (twice the speed of sound) with only about one hundred passengers. The plane had several problems, however: its great speed created high temperatures on its metal skin; its engines were noisy; as it flew faster than sound, a sonic boom split the skies. It did not enter service until 1976. The Boeing 747 jumbo jet made existing technologies bigger, serving about 450 passengers per flight beginning in 1970.

The national airlines of Britain and France operate the Concorde, still the only faster-than-sound passenger craft.

THE TURBOFAN

Jumbo jets had a new type of jet engine, the turbofan. It was similar to a standard jet but with a large, angle-bladed turbine fan at the front. Like a propeller, the fan pushed air backward for added thrust and made the main engine run cooler and more quietly.

large fan to provide extra thrust

turbines to drive compressor and large fan

exhaust

combustion chamber

compressor fan to squash air

Japanese Shinkansen, or "bullet trains," went into service in 1965, almost halving the travel time on some routes.

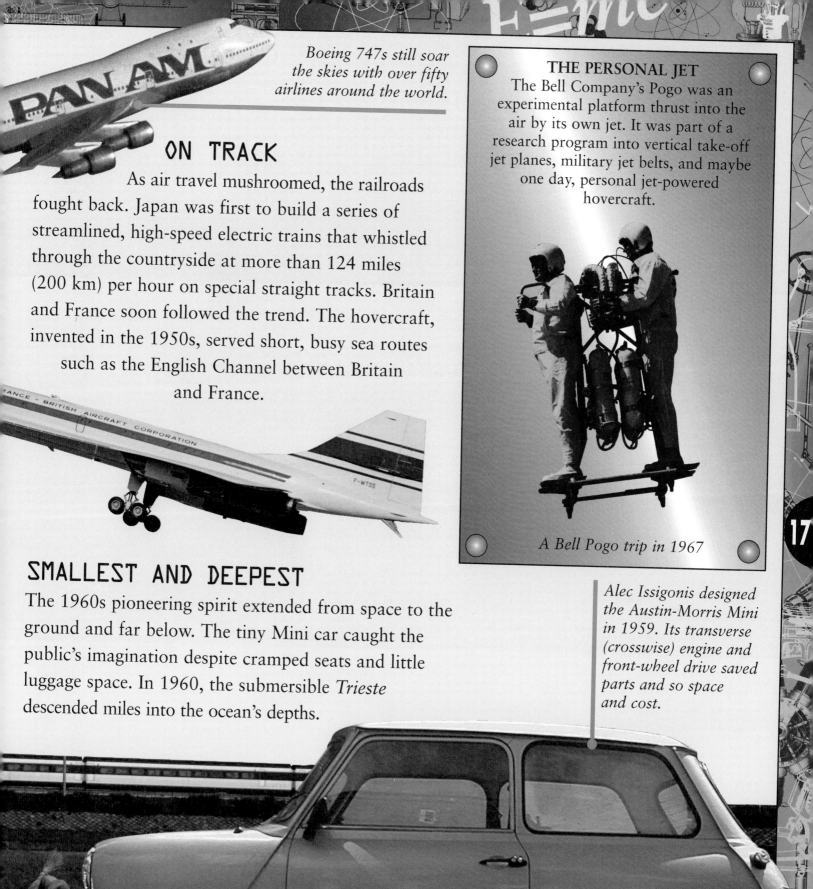

Boeing 747s still soar the skies with over fifty airlines around the world.

ON TRACK

As air travel mushroomed, the railroads fought back. Japan was first to build a series of streamlined, high-speed electric trains that whistled through the countryside at more than 124 miles (200 km) per hour on special straight tracks. Britain and France soon followed the trend. The hovercraft, invented in the 1950s, served short, busy sea routes such as the English Channel between Britain and France.

SMALLEST AND DEEPEST

The 1960s pioneering spirit extended from space to the ground and far below. The tiny Mini car caught the public's imagination despite cramped seats and little luggage space. In 1960, the submersible *Trieste* descended miles into the ocean's depths.

THE PERSONAL JET

The Bell Company's Pogo was an experimental platform thrust into the air by its own jet. It was part of a research program into vertical take-off jet planes, military jet belts, and maybe one day, personal jet-powered hovercraft.

A Bell Pogo trip in 1967

Alec Issigonis designed the Austin-Morris Mini in 1959. Its transverse (crosswise) engine and front-wheel drive saved parts and so space and cost.

ON THE RISE

Unitary technology exploded in the 1960s. All kinds of objects, from plastics to whole skyscrapers, were made from many identical units, or modules.

HOUSES FROM FACTORIES

Inspired by the experimental spirit of the decade, architects and building engineers designed houses based on mass-produced sections or modules. These were made in factories, then quickly plugged together on site. The aim was to manufacture modern, safe, hygienic housing at a low cost.

COLLAPSE!

Unitary or modular building seemed safe if all modules stayed intact to give strength to the whole structure. A small gas explosion in one room of the Ronan Point apartment building collapsed the whole side of the building as if it were made from playing cards. The safety of the modular system was in doubt.

The collapse of Ronan Point, London, 1968.

MASS-PRODUCED LIVING BOXES

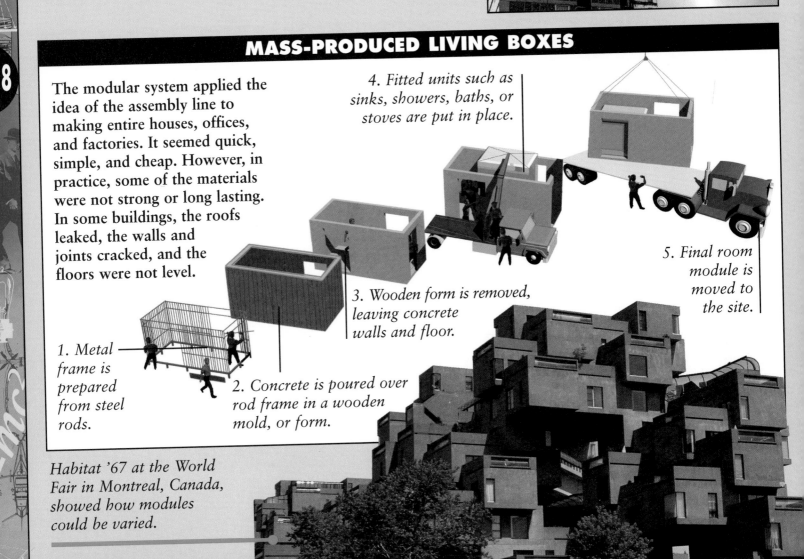

The modular system applied the idea of the assembly line to making entire houses, offices, and factories. It seemed quick, simple, and cheap. However, in practice, some of the materials were not strong or long lasting. In some buildings, the roofs leaked, the walls and joints cracked, and the floors were not level.

4. Fitted units such as sinks, showers, baths, or stoves are put in place.

5. Final room module is moved to the site.

3. Wooden form is removed, leaving concrete walls and floor.

1. Metal frame is prepared from steel rods.

2. Concrete is poured over rod frame in a wooden mold, or form.

Habitat '67 at the World Fair in Montreal, Canada, showed how modules could be varied.

Lake Point Tower in Chicago was completed in 1968. Its sleek, undulating glass walls were based on sketches made in 1921 by Mies van der Rohe, who proposed a curving glass curtain wall — structurally impossible in his time.

LASTING TECHNOLOGY

Modular building used new, strong plastics shaped on production lines. However, many people did not want to live in "little boxes" that were the same as everyone else's homes. A more lasting innovation was the float-glass process for making large sheets of glass quickly and cheaply. Many 1960s skyscrapers look like giant slabs of glass.

FLOAT GLASS

Glass was easy to blow into bottles and similar shapes but difficult to form into large, flat sheets. The float-glass process developed by the 1960s was a great leap forward. Molten or runny glass was spread over a bath of molten tin, heated to more than 446° Fahrenheit (230° Celsius). The glass oozed like syrup to form a ribbon, smooth on top as well as against the mirrorlike surface of the tin beneath it.

Raw glass is mixed.	*Glass melts in oil-fired furnace.*	*Syrupy molten glass floats on tin bath.*	*Glass ribbon is cooled in annealing lehr to make it hard and strong.*	*Sheets are cut from glass ribbon.*	*Sheets are taken to warehouse.*

bath of molten tin / *continuous ribbon of glass*

THE PLASTIC AGE

As more people bought cars and huge trucks carried more goods, the need for gas and diesel fuels rose. These fuels are made from petroleum (crude oil), and some of the by-products of the oil-refining process generated their own industry — plastics.

POLYMERS

Many petrochemical by-products and other substances can be broken down into what chemists call monomer hydrocarbons. These are small molecules containing only hydrogen and carbon. The monomers are then heated and treated to link them together into polymers, like beads in long molecular necklaces, to produce dozens of kinds of plastics.

In the 1960s, designers shaped the new plastics and artificial fibers into exciting fashions. Yves Saint Laurent designed the PVC (polyvinyl chloride) coat in 1966.

MAKING ACRYLIC

Acrylic is the plastic polymer PMMA, polymethyl methacrylate. It can be formed into fibers or into blocks and sheets for all kinds of uses, from signs to aircraft windows.

5. Acrylic fiber is drawn through dryer and then on to be stretched, crimped, and baled.

2. Mix is dissolved in solvent.

4. Liquid acrylic is forced through spinneret into bath to form fiber.

1. Raw ingredients are combined or polymerized.

3. Impurities are filtered out.

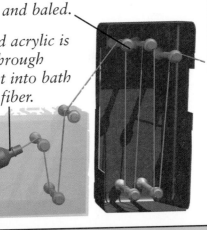

PLASTICS EVERYWHERE

Acrylic-type plastics had first been developed in the 1930s as glasslike sheets. With names such as Perspex and Plexiglass, they were used for high-speed or high-stress applications where glass might shatter, splinter, and cause injury. In the 1960s, acrylic followed rayon and nylon to become the latest, most fashionable artificial fiber. It could be produced in bright colors, drip-dried fast, and needed little care.

The blow chair supposedly spread the body's weight for ultracomfort. However, a tiny pinprick . . .

The transparent TV's Perspex case of 1960 revealed the new transistors and circuits inside.

BECAUSE THEY'RE THERE

The rush to develop new plastics and similar artificial materials led to some unusual products, such as see-through televisions and blow-up furniture. Many of these were designed simply because now they could be.

THE THROWAWAY SOCIETY

During the 1960s, most people were not focusing on the environment and the need to conserve and recycle natural resources. It was a bright, breezy decade of fast fashions and quirky ideas. The same applied to manufacturing. These transparent dresses from 1966 were made of plastic. They were uncomfortable and sticky to wear, but that mattered little. They were designed to be worn once or twice, then thrown away.

Dresses by Hechter of Paris

ELEC-TECH

The space race and military research of the 1960s even improved electrical equipment for the home such as radios and televisions. By 1970, integrated circuits (IC) were replacing transistors, which had been in general use since the early 1950s.

THE MARVELOUS CHIP

An integrated circuit is made with all the transistors, resistors, and other electronic components already in position and connected together, or integrated, instead of manufactured separately and linked by wires. One tiny IC, or chip, contains thousands of such components.

22

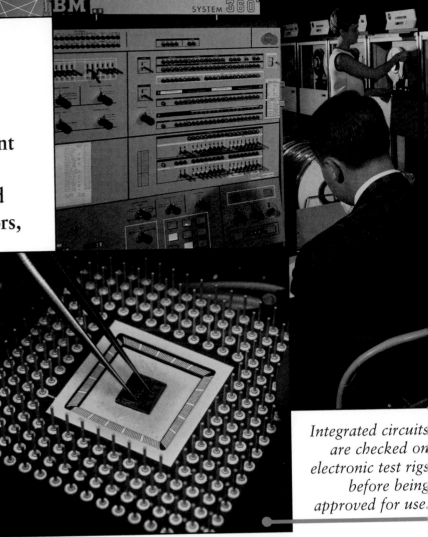

Integrated circuits are checked on electronic test rigs before being approved for use.

Massive trade shows and exhibitions displayed hundreds of radio models.

CHIPS

Integrated circuits are made from semi-conductor materials, such as silicon or germanium, grown in high-pressure vats as lump crystals. Thin wafers are sliced off and cut into chips. Acid or laser light etches or carves components onto the surface of the wafer.

5. chip incorporated into plastic case with connectors

4. wafer cut into chips

3. components printed or etched on wafer

2. silicon wafer

1. silicon crystal

COMPUTERS SHRINK

In the early 1960s, computers were rare and room-sized, found only in government departments, big businesses, and universities. Gradually, they were reduced to the size of filing cabinets. The programs and information were fed in from reels of punched paper tape or magnetic tape; it wasn't until 1967 that people could use typewriter-style keyboards to enter data.

Large reels of magnetic tape dominate the IBM 360 computer room in this 1969 view of the Seabord Coast Line railroad offices, United States.

In-car television was available in 1963, but the car's movements made reception poor, and it was not very popular.

CONSUMER BOOM

During the 1960s, the leading industrial nations grew very wealthy, especially in North America and Europe, as well as in Japan and Australia. People had money to spend, which encouraged new areas of manufacturing. Plastic radios, televisions, vinyl record players, and similar equipment sold in huge numbers.

Mass-pressed vinyl audio discs, called records, boosted the new industry of popular music.

CUTTING EDGE

Lasers are vital in daily life. Different types are used in compact disc players, telephone optical fibers, holograms, medicine, cutting and welding metals, and making microchips and hundreds of other things. This versatile device dates back to 1960, when U.S. physicist Theodore Maiman powered up the first working version.

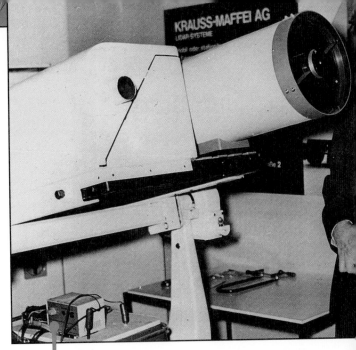

Theodore Maiman (b. 1927) in 1973 with Russian scientist Aleksandr Prokhorov (left). Prokhorov's research helped Maiman build a practical laser.

HOW A LASER WORKS

A laser is based on a substance called the active medium — in Maiman's case, a rod of ruby crystal. A flash tube wrapped around the rod pumps light energy into the crystal. The energy makes atoms in the crystal give off bursts of their own light. These gather together, bounce between mirrors, become stronger, and finally emerge through the partially reflecting mirror.

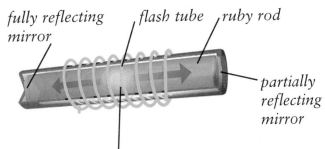

fully reflecting mirror *flash tube* *ruby rod*

partially reflecting mirror

Flash of light from tube gives atoms extra energy.

Atoms give off energy as bursts of light.

Bursts build up and reflect back and forth within rod.

Light escapes through partial mirror as powerful, pure, nonspreading laser beam.

MASERS TO LASERS

The idea behind the laser was not new. A similar device, called a maser, that works with microwaves instead of light waves had been devised in 1954. In 1960, building on other scientists' research, Maiman constructed a powerful light beam of a pure single color that did not spread out.

A scientist tries a laser using gas as the active medium. Laser light waves are all the same length, unlike ordinary light, which has mixed wavelengths.

LASERS EVERYWHERE

Within a year of Maiman's invention, other scientists were developing stronger and more powerful versions and also more delicate and accurate lasers for eye surgery. In 1965, the first holograms were produced using laser light. Holograms are images that can be viewed from different angles to see around and behind objects, yet they are contained on a flat surface. Today, doctors wielding lasers can also help with hearing problems. A tiny bone called the stapes helps transmit vibrations to the inner ear; hardening of the arteries can freeze the stapes in place, completely blocking sound. Previously, surgeons used tiny picks and chisels to free the bones, but now lasers do the job, reducing bleeding and damage to surrounding tissue. Dentists, too, can use lasers to cut out tooth decay or to harden tooth enamel. Plastic surgeons employ lasers to erase tattoos or disfiguring birthmarks with minimal scarring.

THE HOLOGRAM

A holographic image is recorded on photographic film like an ordinary photograph. However, it does not show different colors and shades of light. It shows where two sets of laser light beams come together and interfere or cancel each other out. One set is direct from the laser; the other is reflected from the object.

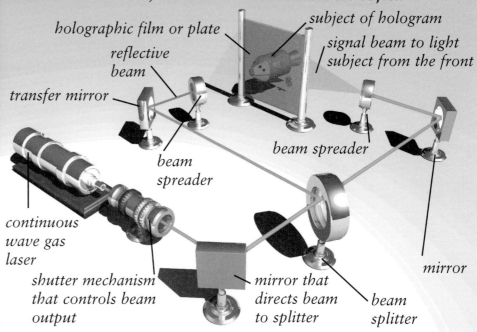

holographic film or plate

subject of hologram

reflective beam

signal beam to light subject from the front

transfer mirror

beam spreader

beam spreader

continuous wave gas laser

shutter mechanism that controls beam output

mirror that directs beam to splitter

beam splitter

mirror

MEDICAL SCIENCE

One of medical history's greatest events took place in Cape Town, South Africa, in 1967 — the first human heart transplant.

A NEW ERA

Chief surgeon for this historic operation was Christiaan Barnard (*b.* 1922). Technically, it was not a demanding or difficult procedure. Its importance lay in the old idea that if the heart stopped, the body was dead. However, medical technology has helped redefine death. In 1966, French doctors were the first to use the idea of brain inactivity instead of a stopped heart as the main sign of death.

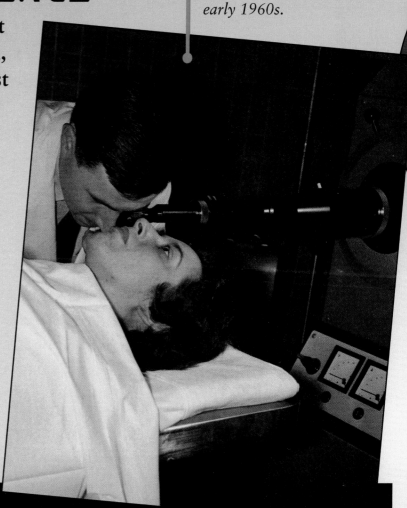

A patient is prepared for laser eye surgery in the early 1960s.

26

LASER EYE SURGERY

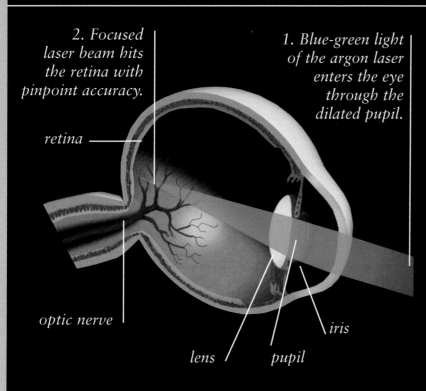

2. Focused laser beam hits the retina with pinpoint accuracy.

1. Blue-green light of the argon laser enters the eye through the dilated pupil.

retina

optic nerve

lens

pupil

iris

One of the first practical uses of laser light was for eye surgery in 1962. With its intense heat, a laser beam could be directed to accurately cut just a tiny area, leaving nearby tissues undamaged. The beam came to a concentrated point, or focus, inside the eye so that it passed through the outer layers without harming them and carried out its work at a precise depth. The beam's heat also welded blood vessels closed so less bleeding occurred than with a scalpel incision. The laser can spot weld a loose or detached retina (the light-sensitive layer) back to the inside of the eyeball.

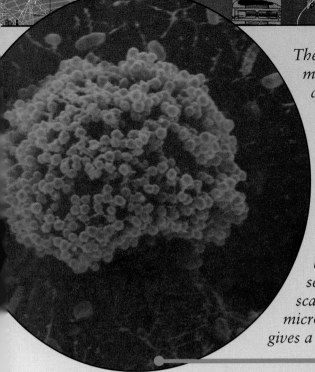

The electron microscope could detect much smaller items than the light microscope.

These small blobs are individual bacteria, seen through a scanning electron microscope that gives a "3-D" view.

SEEING SMALLER

Using beams of electron particles to see tiny objects, the first scanning electron microscopes were developed in 1969. Instead of looking through an object or thin slice, the electron beam scans back and forth across its surface. This provides a more realistic three-dimensional view.

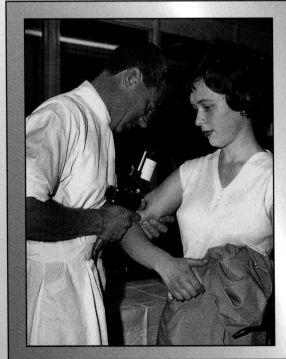

Vaccine by injection

MORE VACCINES

After the success of a vaccine to protect or immunize the body against polio, more vaccines were introduced in the 1960s. They included measles in 1965 and rubella (German measles) in 1969. After a few people fell ill following vaccination, new guidelines were introduced so that people who had certain conditions or a family history of these conditions did not receive the vaccine.

HAVE OR HAVE NOT

The contraceptive pill became available in the early 1960s. It altered the female hormonal cycle to prevent conceiving a baby. In 1967, another hormone-based pill was introduced to do the opposite. Clomiphene, a fertility drug, encouraged a woman's body to produce more ripe eggs, increasing her chances of having a baby.

GADGETS

Most types of electrical appliances designed to take the hard work out of chores, such as washing machines and vacuum cleaners, were well established by the 1960s. The new generation of gadgets focused on increasing convenience, entertainment, leisure, and just plain fun.

SMALLER AND SIMPLER

Shrinking electronics, smaller batteries, plastics, and new methods of mass production made for a whole range of smaller, more portable, hand-held devices. These included radios, tape players, TVs, clocks, and cameras. They were designed to look bright, work quickly, and be simple to operate.

28

The skateboard craze began in 1962 with boards rolling on ball-bearing wheels made of new, soft but tough rubber.

Telephone keypad buttons (1963) worked faster than the usual rotary dial.

TIME FOR ACCURACY

A quartz wristwatch uses quartz (silicon dioxide), the same mineral that forms sand grains. An electric current passing through the quartz makes it oscillate, or vibrate, 32,768 times each second. A microchip counts the vibrations and produces regular pulses of electricity that turn the rotor and the watch hands.

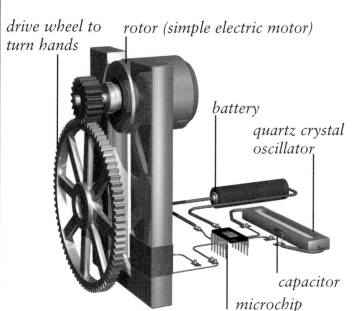

drive wheel to turn hands

rotor (simple electric motor)

battery

quartz crystal oscillator

capacitor

microchip

SMALL MUSIC

Professionals used large reels of magnetic tape to record and play music. In 1963, the Dutch company Philips made a small version for everyday use. The tape reels were protected inside a little case, or "case-ette." Unlike vinyl records, you could record as well as play. This new sound medium was also more convenient than records and less affected by movement.

Cassette tape was too narrow at 1/4 inch (6 millimeters) and moved too slowly past the record/playback head to produce high-quality sound, but it was easy to use and handy to carry.

SNAP-HAPPY

Convenience and *easy to use* were the new catchphrases. Consumer gadgets seemed simple, but their appearance masked sophisticated design and advanced technology. For example, anyone could take snapshots with the Kodak Instamatic. The photos might not be quite up to professional standards but were good enough for most people.

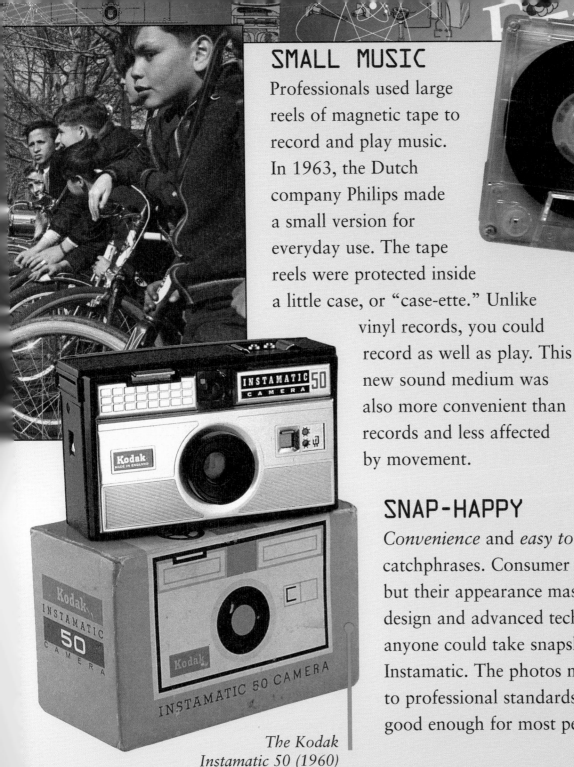

The Kodak Instamatic 50 (1960) turned anyone into a photographer.

THE FINAL WORD

The 1960s produced many conveniences, such as pop-top soda cans and the electric toothbrush. Science and technology, it seemed, could solve any problem; but in the next decade, the effects of new technologies began to appear as pollution and other environmental problems.

Ballpoint and fountain pens had hard, unyielding tips. Felt-tip pens were softer and easier to control.

TIME LINE

	WORLD EVENTS	SCIENCE EVENTS	TECHNOLOGY	FAMOUS SCIENTISTS	INVENTIONS
1960	•Belgian Congo granted independence	•International agreement on defining the meter by the wavelength of a certain kind of light	•U.S. X-15 rocket plane sets air speed record •U.S. nuclear submarine Triton *circumnavigates the world underwater*	•Rudolf Mossbauer discovers the gamma ray effect	•First laser built by Theodore Maiman
1961	•Bay of Pigs invasion of Cuba •Berlin wall built	•Chaos theory is firmly established	•Yuri Gagarin becomes the first person in space •Renault 4 first produced	•Louis and Mary Leakey find fossils of the earliest human, Homo habilis, *in East Africa*	•Electric toothbrush •Barnett Ventilator, a medical electric lung pump
1962	•Cuban Missile Crisis •Algeria gains independence from France	•Telstar 1 *sends on, or relays, live TV broadcast* •A new particle group, hadrons, identified	•U.S. nuclear-powered cargo ship Savannah begins sea trials	•Rachel Carson's book Silent Spring alerts people to chemical pollution	•Silicon breast implant •First commercial skateboards go on sale •U.S.: first industrial robots installed by Unimation
1963	•U.S.: President John F. Kennedy assasinated •U.S.A., USSR, UK sign Nuclear Test Ban Treaty	•Syncom 2 *is first satellite in geosynchronous orbit, staying over same place on Earth*		•Giulo Natta and Karl Ziegler receive the Nobel Prize for their work on polymer plastics	•Philips introduces audio cassette tapes •Friction welding •Measles vaccine
1964	•Vietnam War begins •UN sanctions against South Africa •PLO formed	•U.S. Ranger *probe sends back 4,300 close-up photos of the Moon*	•Verrazano Narrows Bridge, New York, takes record for longest span	•Murray Gell-Mann writes his major account of quarks	•Word processor •Stay-pressed non-iron clothing •Moog synthesizer
1965	•India and Pakistan at war over Kashmir •End of capital punishment in UK	•The planet Venus is discovered to spin in the opposite way from other planets	•Completion of France – Italy road tunnel through Mt. Blanc	•John Kemeny and Thomas Kurtz invent the first computer language for beginners, BASIC	•Widespread use of fertility drugs •Early holograms
1966	•Cultural Revolution in China	•French Academy of Medicine begins to use brain inactivity as an indication of death	•Fast-breeder type of nuclear reactor developed •Luna X is first probe to orbit the Moon	•Konrad Lorenz's book On Aggression *compares the origins of animal and human aggression*	•Fuel-injection engines for cars introduced in UK
1967	•Six-Day War between Israel and Arab nations	•First heart transplant by Christiaan Barnard in South Africa •Pulsars discovered	•U.S. Transit system becomes first satellite navigation method	•Arthur Kornberg and his team are the first to copy DNA in the laboratory	•Dolby invents noise reduction system for stereos •Mammography for detecting breast cancer
1968	•USSR invades Czechoslovakia •U.S. civil rights leader Martin Luther King, Jr. shot	•Apollo 8 goes to the Moon, orbits ten times, and returns safely	•Aswan Dam completed •Collapse at Ronan Point	•Joseph Weber reports first finding of theoretical gravitational waves; not many take him seriously	•First oil-carrying supertankers •Radiation (waves) to sterilize and preserve foods
1969	•Neil Armstrong: first moon walk •Concorde's first flight •Several terrorist groups "skyjack" airliners	•The world watches on live TV as Neil Armstrong becomes first person to walk on the Moon	•Hurricane Debbie is weakened by "seeding" with silver iodide crystals	•Jonathan Beckwith and his team isolate the first single gene	•Home yogurt-makers •Bubble memory for computers

GLOSSARY

atom: the smallest part of a pure substance (chemical element) that can naturally exist. Most atoms are made of three types of even tinier particles called protons, neutrons, and electrons.

DNA: the chemical substance that contains, in the form of a code, the instructions or genes for living things to grow and survive. DNA stands for de-oxyribonucleic acid.

integrated circuit: a small device that contains many electronic components, such as transistors, resistors and capacitors, already linked or integrated into whole pathways or circuits.

laser: a device that produces waves of intense, powerful, high-energy, pure-color light. The term is an acronym for Light Amplification by Stimulated Emission of Radiation.

polymer: a substance whose molecules, or chemical building parts, are made of identical units, called monomers, that are joined like beads in a necklace or bricks in a wall.

quark: one of the smallest pieces of matter, an elementary or fundamental particle. Quarks of various types and combinations make up slightly larger particles such as protons and neutrons, which in turn are parts of atoms.

quasar: a region of space that gives off more energy than almost any other. It perhaps consists of an entire galaxy falling into a giant black hole.

space probe: an unmanned craft that travels into space, usually to fly near or land on another planet, a moon or, in the case of Giotto, a comet.

unitary (modular) construction: a type of construction that utilizes many similar parts, units, or modules.

MORE BOOKS TO READ

Great Discoveries & Inventions That Advanced Industry and Technology. Great Discoveries and Inventions (series). Antonio Casanellas (Gareth Stevens)

How Did We Find Out About Lasers? How Did We Find Out-? (series). Isaac Asimov (Walker & Co.)

Medical Advances. 20th Century Inventions (series). Steve Parker (Raintree/Steck Vaughn)

One Giant Leap: The First Moon Landing. Smithsonian Odyssey (series). Dana Meachen Rau (Soundprints Corp. Audio)

Plastics and Polymers. Everyday Material Science Experiments (series). Robert C. Mebane and Thomas R. Rybolt (Twenty First Century Books)

The Race to Space. Giant Leaps (series). Stuart A. Kallen (Abdo & Daughters)

Radio Astronomy. Above and Beyond (series). Adele D. Richardson (Smart Apple Media)

The World of Atoms and Quarks. Scientific American Sourcebooks (series). Albert Stwertka (Twenty First Century Books)

31

WEB SITES

Cut to the Heart.
www.pbs.org/wgbh/nova/heart

I Can Do That!: The Fun Science Site.
www.eurekascience.com/ICanDoThat/index.htm

NASA for Kids.
www.nasa.gov/kids.html

NOVA Online: The Atom Builder.
www.pbs.org/wgbh/nova/diamond/insideparticles.html

Due to the dynamic nature of the Internet, some web sites stay current longer than others. To find additional web sites, use a reliable search engine with one or more of the following keywords: *John Glenn, lasers, lunar modules, NASA, quasars, satellites,* Saturn V *rocket, Alan Shepherd, space race,* and Sputnik.

INDEX